THE
VICTORIAN KITCHEN
Book of
PICKLES & PRESERVES

THE
VICTORIAN KITCHEN
Book of
PICKLES AND PRESERVES

JG PRESS

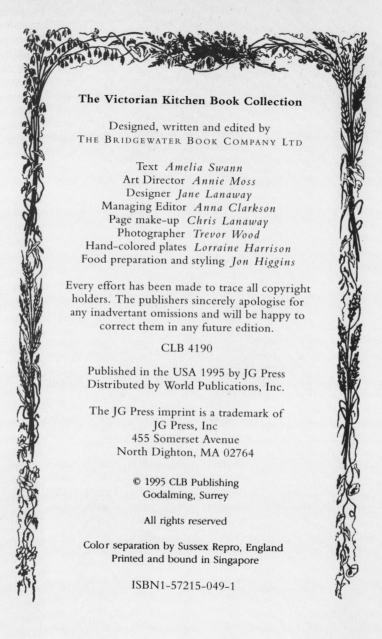

The Victorian Kitchen Book Collection

Designed, written and edited by
THE BRIDGEWATER BOOK COMPANY LTD

Text *Amelia Swann*
Art Director *Annie Moss*
Designer *Jane Lanaway*
Managing Editor *Anna Clarkson*
Page make-up *Chris Lanaway*
Photographer *Trevor Wood*
Hand-colored plates *Lorraine Harrison*
Food preparation and styling *Jon Higgins*

Every effort has been made to trace all copyright
holders. The publishers sincerely apologise for
any inadvertant omissions and will be happy to
correct them in any future edition.

CLB 4190

Published in the USA 1995 by JG Press
Distributed by World Publications, Inc.

The JG Press imprint is a trademark of
JG Press, Inc
455 Somerset Avenue
North Dighton, MA 02764

Color separation by Sussex Repro, England
Printed and bound in Singapore

ISBN1-57215-049-1

CONTENTS

INTRODUCTION

Eliza Acton

Pickles are as old as the Greeks and Romans. The pickling process was a way to preserve perishable food for winter or times of shortage, or for traveling or export. Although most modern pickles are based on vegetables, the gourmets of the ancient world also enjoyed fish and meat pickled in brine or vinegar with spices. The spices and vinegar involved in the process also made food safer to eat than it might have been in its raw state.

By the 19th century, commercial pickles were widely available, and as economical to buy as to make at home. However, Mrs. Beeton advised that "all housewives who have sufficient time and convenience" should make their own. Eliza Acton had rather a low opinion of pickles, which she considered,

> *Pickling is so easy a process... that when in any degree properly aquired, it may be extended to almost every kind of fruit and vegetable successfully.*

ELIZA ACTON'S PICKLING HINTS

Here are Eliza Acton's tips for successful pickling, rendered into modern English.

1 **Always use the best vinegar – preferably French.**
2 **Keep the pickles entirely covered in their liquid.**
3 **Do not let air or damp near your pickles.**

WARNING!

Never let metal come into contact with pickles. If you need to strain your pickle or vinegar, use a nylon sieve.

with some exceptions, to be "not very wholesome articles of diet." She abhorred "bought pickle" as "eminently dangerous to persons who partake of them often and largely," and also advised that pickles should be homemade. Flavored vinegars and mustards were to be preferred, but she suggests that mushrooms, Indian mangoes, walnuts, gherkins, lemons, shallots, and peaches made the most digestible pickle.

The recipes in this book can only suggest the huge range of pickles, savory vinegars, store sauces, and preserved meat prepared by Victorian cooks and housewives. The recipes are based on authentic Victorian sources, but, of course, many of these are in turn founded on timeless, traditional methods.

STORE SAUCES

These were made by Victorian cooks to keep in the pantry for the flavoring of gravies, stews, salad dressings, and more complicated sauces.

Potted Meats

The potted meats and fish of today, served in tiny ramekins with a thin skim of butter and token parsley garnish, are a feeble echo of the mighty pots of meat made for seafarers to take with them on long voyages under sail. Only the best parts of the meat were used, pounded and mixed with fat and spices, tightly packed, and covered with a stout, airtight seal of suet or a thick layer of butter. Herbs were laid across the top to keep off flies. As much as 16lb. of meat could be potted up in this way.

PREPARING THE JARS

ALWAYS STERILIZE JARS AND BOTTLES, AND USE ACID-PROOF LIDS. YOU CAN BUY DISCS OF VINEGAR-PROOF CARDBOARD DESIGNED FOR THE PURPOSE. SCREW-TOP LIDS ARE BEST; SAVE BOTTLES AND JARS FROM COMMERCIALLY BOUGHT PRODUCTS FOR YOUR OWN PICKLES. REMEMBER TO LABEL AND DATE YOUR PICKLES AS SOON AS THEY ARE MADE - AFTER A FEW MONTHS' STORAGE, MANY ARE DIFFICULT TO IDENTIFY FROM COLOR ALONE.

EVERYTHING YOU NEED FOR PICKLING AND
PRESERVING IN THE VICTORIAN STYLE

PICKLED LEMONS

This is based on Mrs. Beeton's recipe. Unlike Lemon Pickle, the lemons are left whole to be eaten as a relish with meat and fish. They should be left to marinate for at least three months before eating, but will keep for up to a year.

INGREDIENTS

6 Fresh Lemons

Salt

5 cups Vinegar

1/8 cup Whole Cloves

1/8 cup White Peppercorns

Small Piece of Fresh Root Ginger

Piece of Cinnamon Stick

2 Cloves Garlic

Salt

METHOD

❧ In a large bowl mix up a strong salt solution using freshly drawn water. Place the lemons in the liquid and allow to soak for approximately seven days, stirring occasionally.

❧ When the lemons feel soft, remove them from the solution and wipe them to remove any excess salt. Pack them into a large, wide-necked jar. Meanwhile, bring the vinegar and spices to a boil in a saucepan and allow to cool for approximately one hour before pouring through muslin.

❧ Reboil the strained, spiced vinegar and pour over the lemons, covering them completely. Cover with a waxed disc and seal tightly.

The Reverend and the Lemon

The Reverend Sydney Smith (1771–1845), a witty and welcome guest at the tables of the great, was probably the first known "foodie." Because of his radical views, he was sent to an obscure parish in Yorkshire, "so far out of the way it was actually 12 miles from a lemon!" The resourceful Reverend contrived a substitute using lemon essence and citric acid.

LEMON PICKLE

This tangy pickle is a treat for those with a taste for tart relishes. It is very good with fried fish. Use a little of the pickle juice to flavor white sauces for fish or poultry.

INGREDIENTS

6 Fresh Juicy Lemons

2½ cups Vinegar

2 T. Salt

Pinch of Saffron

Pinch of Cayenne Pepper

2 Whole Cloves

METHOD

❧ Leaving their skins on, chop the lemons into small pieces, removing any seeds. Place the pieces in a jar with half the vinegar and all the remaining ingredients except the cayenne, and cover with a waxed disc.

❧ Place in a low oven for about three hours so the fruit can stew. When the lemon pieces are tender, pour off the liquid. Add the remaining vinegar and cayenne pepper, bring to the boil and pour over the lemon pieces, ensuring they are fully covered.

❧ Cover and seal the jar tightly.

LEMON BRANDY

This is another great idea from Eliza Acton. She suggests that you might add a few blanched apricot kernels for an "agreeable flavour." Lemon Brandy is excellent for flavoring sweet dishes and whipped cream. It is perhaps advisable to mark the bottle after each use, too!

INGREDIENTS

6 Fresh Lemons

Half a Bottle of Good Brandy

METHOD

❧ Using a zester, remove the rind from the six lemons and place in a jar with a tight-fitting lid, pour over the brandy and seal tightly.

❧ Allow approximately two weeks for the lemon zests to infuse before straining off the spirit and returning to its original bottle.

JUICY LEMONS RIPE FOR PICKLING OR
PRESERVING IN BRANDY

SWEET BASIL VINEGAR

—❧—

This is based on Eliza Acton's recipe. It is a useful and attractive way to capture the summery pungency of basil. Stand your filled bottle on a sunny shelf to encourage the basil to infuse. Use Sweet Basil Vinegar in salad dressings, or sprinkle onto fresh tomatoes served with olive oil.

INGREDIENTS

Good Handful of Fresh Basil
2 ½ cups Pale Vinegar

—❧—

METHOD

❧ Wash the basil under fresh running water and bruise the leaves, with the heel of a knife to allow the distinctive qualities of the herb to infuse.

❧ Place the basil in a clean, wide-necked bottle and pour over the vinegar. Seal tightly and leave for two to three weeks, but no longer. It is advisable to strain off and rebottle the vinegar at this point, as the basil flavor may be a little over-powering for some tastes.

GREEN MINT VINEGAR

—❧—

This is from Eliza Acton. Like Mint Jelly, it is an excellent way of putting to good use the profligate amount of mint that most herb gardens produce. To keep the color refreshingly green, use only young leaves.

INGREDIENTS

Plenty of Fresh Mint
2 ½ cups Pale Vinegar

—❧—

METHOD

❧ Carefully wash the mint, pluck the leaves from the stalks, and roughly chop.

❧ Fill glass jars almost to neck level with the mint, pour over the vinegar, and seal tightly.

❧ After three weeks, strain the vinegar through muslin and bottle for future use.

And she forgot the stars, the moon, and sun,
And she forgot the blue above the trees
And she forgot the dells where waters run,
And she forgot the chilly autumn breeze;
She had no knowledge whan the day was done,
And the new morn she saw not: but in peace
Hung over her sweet Basil evermore,
And moisten'd it with tears unto the core.

JOHN KEATS,
Isabella; OR, the Pot of Basil

TARRAGON VINEGAR

*T*his is based on Eliza Acton's
instructions. She recommends that you pick the tarragon just before
it blossoms, in July or August. It makes a strong but agreeable
vinegar and "imparts quite a foreign character to the dishes for
which it is used."
You can use it to make Tartar Sauce for fish; it also
tastes good with chicken.

INGREDIENTS

Bunch of Fresh Tarragon
5 cups White Wine Vinegar

METHOD

❦ Wash the tarragon thoroughly and bruise the leaves with the heel of
a kitchen knife to release their unique flavor and smell.

❦ Place the leaves in clean glass bottles and pour over the wine
vinegar. Cork and allow to stand for at least two months before use, or
longer if you like.

❦ Strain off, pour into small bottles, and cork them well. You could
put a sprig of fresh tarragon in each bottle for decorative purposes.

A SELECTION OF PUNGENT AND COLORFUL
HERB VINEGARS

CELERY VINEGAR

This is based on one of Eliza Acton's many recipes for flavored vinegar. It can be strained off and bottled after three or four weeks, but you can safely leave the celery in the jar for three or four months, if desired. Celery Vinegar can be used to flavor soups or stews, or used directly as a condiment.

INGREDIENTS

3¾ cups White Wine Vinegar
Head of Celery
2 T. Black Peppercorns
2 T. Salt

METHOD

❧ Pour the vinegar into a saucepan and add the peppercorns and salt. Bring to the boil and add the celery, finely chopped. Continue boiling for three minutes to allow the celery to soften slightly.

❧ Remove from the heat, pour the whole contents of the pan into a clean jar, and allow to cool. Seal the jar tightly and put away for three weeks to allow the celery to impart its flavor.

❧ When ready for bottling, pour the vinegar through a muslin to leave a clear, subtle-tasting vinegar that will keep for several months without deterioration.

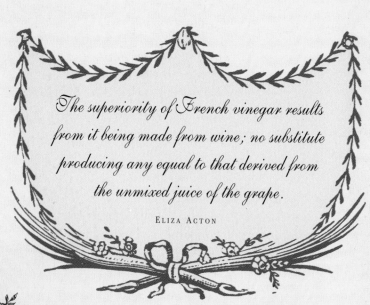

The superiority of French vinegar results from it being made from wine; no substitute producing any equal to that derived from the unmixed juice of the grape.

ELIZA ACTON

HORSERADISH VINEGAR

This is based on a recipe from Mrs. Beeton. The vinegar can be used immediately it has been prepared — although it will keep for some months — and makes an excellent relish for cold meat, particularly cold roast beef.

INGREDIENTS

Small Piece Fresh Horseradish Root
Good Pinch of Mustard Powder
2½ cups Vinegar

METHOD

❧ Finely grate the horseradish and place in a sealable jar along with the mustard powder and vinegar. Seal tightly and give it a good shake.

❧ Shake the jar vigorously once a day for at least fourteen days so that the earthy flavor of the horseradish is thoroughly infused.

❧ Pour the finished vinegar through muslin and bottle. Seal tightly.

ROOT VEGETABLES TO MAKE AROMATIC
AND UNUSUAL VINEGARS

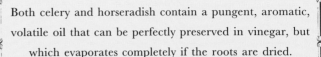

Both celery and horseradish contain a pungent, aromatic, volatile oil that can be perfectly preserved in vinegar, but which evaporates completely if the roots are dried. Horseradish contains a powerful antibiotic that protects the intestinal tract; in Japan, it is served with raw fish to counteract any gastric unpleasantness.

CHILI VINEGAR

This is Mrs. Beeton's recipe. She considered it to be an "agreeable relish to fish, as many people cannot eat it without the addition of an acid." This is a particularly attractive flavored vinegar and makes for an impressive sight in any kitchen; therefore, leave the bright chilies in the vinegar while in use.

COOK'S TIP

Chillies are a very powerful irritant to skin and eyes. When cutting them, be very careful not to get any juice on your skin or into your eyes. If you do, wash off with plenty of cold water immediately.

INGREDIENTS

15 Fresh Red Chilies
2 1/2 cups White Wine Vinegar

METHOD

❦ Cut the chillies in half lengthways and place in a wide-mouthed bottle. Pour over the vinegar and allow to infuse for at least fourteen days before use.

ESCHALOT WINE

This is based on Eliza Acton's recipe; eschalots are what we call shallots. She considered it a "useful preparation," as it could be used to give a shallot flavor to dishes "that did not require acid." It can also be used to make a robust salad dressing.

INGREDIENTS

1 cup Shallots
2 1/2 cups Medium Sherry

METHOD

❦ Peel and bruise the shallots, and place them in a wide-mouthed bottle. Pour over the sherry and seal tightly.
❦ Allow to infuse for approximately fourteen days, shaking the bottle daily for the first twelve days, but leaving untouched for the last two. This allows any sediment to fall to the bottom of the bottle.
❦ Carefully pour off the sherry for rebottling. The liquid will be clear if you have let the sediment settle properly.

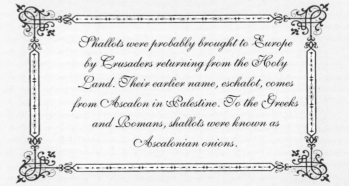

Shallots were probably brought to Europe by Crusaders returning from the Holy Land. Their earlier name, eschalot, comes from Ascalon in Palestine. To the Greeks and Romans, shallots were known as Ascalonian onions.

A dog, a steak and a walnut tree
The more you beat 'em, the better they be.

ANON

PICKLED WALNUTS

This is based on Eliza Acton's recipe, but pickled walnuts have been a part of the English kitchen for centuries. If you want to eat the walnuts as soon as they are made, leave them soaking in brine for an extra four days before beginning the pickling process. Pickled Walnuts were traditionally packed in stone jars.

WALNUTS, A FAVORITE WITH THE VICTORIANS, WHETHER FRESH, PICKLED, OR PRESERVED

COOK'S TIP

The walnuts should be full grown, but green and soft. They are at their best in July. Test for texture by running the head of a needle through the nut. Some recipes suggest you prick them all over, but this breaks the skin and makes them look ragged.

INGREDIENTS

4 cups Green Walnuts
$2/3$ cup Salt
$7^{1}/2$ cups Vinegar
$1/3$ cup Black Pepper
Small Piece Fresh Stem Ginger
2 T. Cloves
$1/3$ cup Mustard Seed
1t. Salt (for Vinegar)

METHOD

❧ To ensure only the freshest of walnuts are being used, prick them all with a pin or needle. Any that feel hard should be discarded, as they are past their best for pickling. Make a solution with half of the salt and $2^{1}/2$ cups of fresh cold water, add the walnuts, and allow to soak for four days, stirring once or twice a day.

❧ Repeat this process with the remainder of the salt and allow the walnuts to soak for another four days. After this time, remove the nuts from the water, spread them on a tray, and leave them exposed to the air to blacken. Turn them a few times to make sure they go an even black all over, then pack them into jars.

❧ Boil the vinegar and the remaining ingredients together for five minutes and pour over the walnuts, making sure that they are fully immersed. Cover and seal tightly when cold.

WALNUT KETCHUP

This is from Mrs. Beeton's recipe; she notes that "if required a little more vinegar or port can be added." It makes a tasty addition to rich beef stews, chops, or steaks.

INGREDIENTS

4 cups Green Walnuts	Ginger
$1/8$ cup Salt	10 Peeled Shallots
$2^{1}/2$ cups Vinegar	Can of Anchovies
Good Pinch of Ground	(Well-Drained)
Mace, Nutmeg, Cloves,	$1^{3}/4$ cups Port

METHOD

❧ To ensure the walnuts are in perfect condition for this vinegar, spike them all with a pin first. Any that are difficult to spike should be discarded. Gently bruise the remaining walnuts with the heel of a kitchen knife and place in a jar with the salt and vinegar.

❧ Seal the jar well and put to one side for seven days, shaking or stirring well each day. Then pour off the liquid and bring it to the boil.

❧ Add the rest of the above ingredients and continue to boil for 30 minutes to allow all the flavors to blend thoroughly. Do not strain the vinegar before bottling.

When Mrs. Beeton was writing, tomatoes were rarely eaten as a salad vegetables, but *"chiefly used in soups, sauces and gravies."* They were also served cooked as an accompaniment to meat, and, *"in its unripe state, esteemed as an excellent sauce for roast goose or pork."*

BOTTLED TOMATOES

This is a recipe adapted from Eliza Acton's original "Bottled Tomatas, or Tomata Catsup." The recipe was given by "a person who makes by it every year large quantities of the catsup, which is considered excellent."

INGREDIENTS

5lb. Fresh Ripe Tomatoes	Handful of Fresh Oregano
2 large Onions	Salt and Black Pepper
⅔ cup Good-Quality Oil	½ cup Sugar
⅔ cup Sweet Basil Vinegar (see page 10)	

METHOD

❧ Roughly chop the tomatoes and place in a saucepan over a very low heat until they cook down to a pulp. Press through a sieve to remove all skin and seeds.

❧ Chop the onions and fry in the oil until soft but not colored. Add the rest of the ingredients and the tomato pulp, mixing thoroughly. Cook over a low heat for 30 minutes, until the mixture has thickened considerably and taken on a lovely, glossy appearance.

❧ Pour the tomato sauce into warm, sterilized jars while still hot, and seal well.

TOMATO SAUCE

This is based on Mrs. Beeton's recipe for Tomato Sauce for Keeping. As she observed, the sauce "will keep good for two or three years, but will be fit for use in a week."

INGREDIENTS

5lb. Fresh Ripe Tomatoes	Good Pinch of Salt
2½ cups Chili Vinegar (see page 13)	⅔ cup Soy Sauce
¼ cup Chopped Onion	⅔ cup Fish Sauce to Keep (see page 25)
4 Cloves of Garlic	

METHOD

❧ Roughly chop the tomatoes and garlic and place in a saucepan with the chili vinegar, onion, and salt. Bring to the boil and cook until the onion and garlic have softened.

❧ Remove from the heat and press the contents of the pan through a sieve, then return the sauce to the heat and bring back to a boil. Add the soy sauce and anchovy essence/fish sauce, and allow to continue boiling for 20 minutes until thickened.

❧ Bottle and seal tightly.

MUSHROOM KETCHUP

Mushroom ketchup was a mainstay of the Victorian cook's pantry. Both Mrs. Beeton and Eliza Acton have recipes; Eliza Acton calls hers Mushroom Catsup. Mrs. Beeton considered it "one of the most useful store sauces to the experienced cook, and no trouble should be spared in its preparation."

This sauce keeps for a year, at least. It is the basis for the concentrated Double Mushroom Ketchup.

INGREDIENTS

4lb. Fresh Mushrooms
½ cup Salt
Good Pinch of Cayenne Pepper Allspice
Ground Ginger
3 T. Brandy (optional)

METHOD

❧ In a good-sized saucepan, alternately layer mushrooms and salt until all are used. Put to one side for two to three days, stirring and mashing the mixture regularly to allow all the juices to be extracted from the mushrooms.

❧ After three days, strain the juices into a saucepan and allow to boil for 15 minutes before adding the spices.

❧ Continue boiling for a further 20 minutes, then remove from the heat and allow to cool completely before bottling. A few drops of good brandy can be added to each bottle of ketchup at this stage, if desired. Seal the bottles tightly.

MUSHROOMS MAKE A CHEAP, YET DELICIOUS,
SAUCE TO FLAVOR MEAT DISHES

DOUBLE MUSHROOM KETCHUP

Both Mrs. Beeton and Eliza Acton have recipes for this concentrated sauce. Mrs. Beeton pointed out that it was very economical in use, as a little goes a long way. It keeps very well, and is an invaluable addition to gravies and sauces for any meat dish.

INGREDIENTS

4lb. Fresh mushrooms
¼ cup salt
2½ cups Ready-Made Mushroom Ketchup
2 T. Whole Black Peppercorns
¼ cup Ground Ginger

METHOD

❦ Put the mushrooms in a large saucepan and strew the salt over the top of them. Pour over the mushroom ketchup and stir together to mix thoroughly.

❦ Put the saucepan to one side for three days, stirring occasionally to allow the juices to be extracted from the fresh mushrooms.

❦ After three days, pour the liquor off into a saucepan and boil it for fifteen minutes with the peppercorns and ground ginger. Allow the ketchup to cool completely before bottling and sealing tightly.

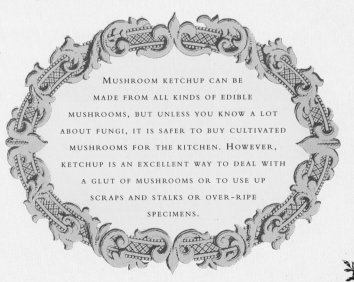

MUSHROOM KETCHUP CAN BE
MADE FROM ALL KINDS OF EDIBLE
MUSHROOMS, BUT UNLESS YOU KNOW A LOT
ABOUT FUNGI, IT IS SAFER TO BUY CULTIVATED
MUSHROOMS FOR THE KITCHEN. HOWEVER,
KETCHUP IS AN EXCELLENT WAY TO DEAL WITH
A GLUT OF MUSHROOMS OR TO USE UP
SCRAPS AND STALKS OR OVER-RIPE
SPECIMENS.

THE INFLUENCE OF THE RAJ

In 1858, the British took over as rulers of India from the East India Company, which had been the controlling force in the country since 1757. The British Parliament assumed direct control over 11 provinces – called British India – and indirect control over the rest of the country, known as the Indian States, which were ruled by puppet Indian princes. France and Portugal maintained a toehold on some of the coastal strip. Queen Victoria became Empress of India in 1871. A huge bureaucracy mushroomed to administer this Empire, the British Raj, and a large army installed to deal with rebellion. Soldiers and civil servants flocked to India, taking their wives and families with them; when they returned, they brought with them a taste for the curries and chutneys that they had eaten there, and tried to recreate them at home.

BENGAL RECIPE FOR MANGO CHUTNEY

This is adapted from a recipe collected by Mrs. Beeton. She reports that it was given "by a native" to an English lady living in India, and that this lady brought it to England, where she became "quite celebrated amongst her friends for the excellence of this Eastern relish." The original recipe used unripe mangoes instead of apples. Mrs. Beeton also noted that the chutney "is very superior to any which can be bought, and one trial will prove it to be delicious."

INGREDIENTS

5lb. Unripe Cooking Apples
1 3/4 cups Moist Brown Sugar
1/2 cup Salt
1/3 cup Crushed Garlic Cloves
1/3 cup Finely Chopped Onion
1 1/3 cups Powdered Ginger
1/4 cup Chopped Fresh Red Chilies
1/4 cup Mustard Seed
1 cup Seedless Raisins
5 cups Malt Vinegar

METHOD

❧ Peel, core, and slice the apples and place in a saucepan along with the vinegar. Bring to the boil and simmer until the apples are tender, but do not allow them to break up.

❧ Pound the garlic, onions, ginger, and mustard seed in a mortar and pestle and add to the apple mixture along with the sugar, which should be dissolved in 2 cups of boiling water. Stirring well, add the remaining ingredients and allow to simmer gently for ten minutes to infuse the flavors.

❧ Spoon the chutney into warm, sterilized jars and seal tightly.

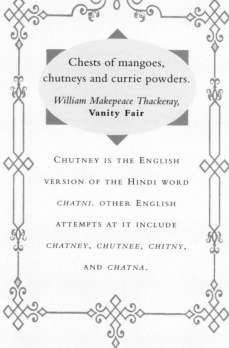

Chests of mangoes, chutneys and currie powders.

William Makepeace Thackeray, **Vanity Fair**

CHUTNEY IS THE ENGLISH VERSION OF THE HINDI WORD *CHATNI.* OTHER ENGLISH ATTEMPTS AT IT INCLUDE *CHATNEY, CHUTNEE, CHITNY,* AND *CHATNA.*

SQUASH MANGOES

This is a recipe from 1850, collected from London's East India Dock. The marrow squash had just been introduced to England, and ways of using it were still being explored. The "mango" process had been popular since the 18th century, when the mango had first come to England. It became fashionable to try to make ingenious imitations. Melon mangoes, made on the same principle, were also popular.

INGREDIENTS

1 Small Marrow Squash
1/4 cup Mustard Seed
6 Cloves Garlic, Peeled and Sliced
1/2 cup Fresh Horseradish Root, Grated
Pickling Spices
2 1/2 cups Vinegar
1/4 cup Sugar

METHOD

❧ Cut the marrow squash in half lengthways and remove all the seeds. Lay both halves in a pan of salted water and leave overnight. The following day, remove the squash and drain off as much liquid as possible, then pack the cavity with all the remaining ingredients, except the sugar, and tie the two halves back together again.

❧ Place the squash into a large jar or pot. Boil the vinegar, pour it over the squash, and allow to stand for 24 hours. The following day, drain off the liquid, reheat, and pour over once more. This process should be repeated until the squash looks dark and soft. When it does, untie the squash, remove the "stuffing," and slice the flesh thinly. Pack into sterilized jars.

❧ Reboil the vinegar with the sugar and pour into the jars, ensuring the squash slices are fully covered. Seal the jars. Leave for 2 months before consuming.

MELONS, MARROWS, AND PEACHES MAKE
SPICY CHUTNEYS AND TANGY "MANGOES."

PEACH MANGOES

This is based on Eliza Acton's instructions for
the conversion of Pickled Peaches into Peach Mangoes.
They can be served on occasions when you might serve
actual mangoes, and so go well with light curry dishes.

INGREDIENTS

6 Pickled Peaches (see page 29)

¼ cup Mustard Seed

4 Cloves Garlic, Peeled

¼ cup Cayenne Pepper

¼ cup Ground Cinnamon

2 Red Chilies, Seeded and Sliced

METHOD

❧ Remove the Pickled Peaches from their brine and cut
the top from each fruit to allow the stone to be removed.
Reserve the "lids."

❧ Pound the remaining ingredients in a mortar and
pestle and fill each stone cavity with the mixture.
Replace the lid, tying it on if necessary.

CHATNEY SAUCE

This is based on Eliza Acton's "Bengal Receipt."
Her original suggested crab apples or unripe bullaces (damsons),
although she had reservations about the use of such hard,
acid fruits, which she considered bad for the digestion. Lightly
warmed tomatoes or gooseberries could be substituted for the
apples. Chatney Sauce should have a thick, creamy consistency.

INGREDIENTS

½ lb. Cooking Apples

½ cup Seedless Raisins

½ cup Soft Brown Sugar

1¾ cups Malt Vinegar

½ cup Ground Ginger

⅛ cup Salt

⅛ cup Cayenne Pepper

¼ cup Ground Coriander

METHOD

❧ Peel, core, and roughly chop the cooking apples, and place in a
saucepan with the rest of the ingredients. Mix together well and bring
to the boil.

❧ Reduce the heat to a simmer and cook the chutney until it becomes
thick and pulpy. Bruise some cloves of garlic and drop one into each
warm, sterilized jar, pack the jars with chutney, and seal.

PICKLED GHERKINS

Gherkins are immature cucumbers with little flavor, so they make very good pickles. This is based on Mrs. Beeton's recipe. She pointed out that "as a pickle, they are a very general favourite."

INGREDIENTS

1lb. Gherkins
¼ cup Salt
Small Piece of Fresh Ginger
2½ cups Vinegar

1 t. Whole Black Peppercorns
1 t. Whole Allspice
2 Cloves

METHOD

❦ Dissolve the salt in 2½ cups of cold water and pour into a bowl. Add the gherkins and leave to soak. Remove them after three days, pat them dry with a clean cloth, and place them in a sterilized jar.

❦ Pour the vinegar into a saucepan and add the remaining ingredients, bring to the boil, and allow to simmer for ten minutes while the spices infuse. Strain the boiling vinegar over the gherkins and cover the jar tightly. Allow to stand for 24 hours.

❦ On the next day, drain off the vinegar and reboil. Pour over the gherkins once more and seal tightly. Allow 6 to 8 weeks before eating.

PICKLED GHERKINS: THE IDEAL ACCOMPANIMENT TO BREAD AND CHEESE

MIXED PICKLE

INGREDIENTS

6½ cups Mixed Cauliflower Florets, Peeled Small Onions, Sliced Cucumber, Gherkins, Seeded and Sliced Peppers, Trimmed French Beans
5 cups Vinegar
¼ cup Ground Ginger
¼ cup Mustard Powder
⅛ cup Salt
2 T. Mustard Seed
Pinch of Cayenne Pepper

Every self-respecting Victorian cook, housekeeper, and housewife had her own recipe for mixed pickle, often handed down through the family. Pickling surplus vegetables was a serious operation. This is adapted from Mrs. Beeton's "very good" recipe.

METHOD

❦ Thoroughly wash the prepared vegetables and pat dry with a clean cloth. Pack them into sterilized jars.

❦ Place the spices in a bowl with a small amount of vinegar and mix to a smooth paste. Add this paste to the rest of the vinegar. Bring the mixture to the boil and simmer for a few minutes before removing from the heat and cooling completely.

❦ Pour the cooled vinegar into the jars. Make sure you cover the vegetables completely. Seal tightly.

ALL THE INGREDIENTS FOR A SERIOUS PICKLING OPERATION

EXCELLENT PICKLE

This is from Mrs. Beeton's recipe. The pickle can be eaten the day it is made, but it looks so good in its jar that it seems a pity to spoil it. An elegant, simple pickle, excellent for giving as a present.

INGREDIENTS

1 lb. Cucumber	Cayenne Pepper
1 lb. Cooking Apples	²/₃ cup Soy Sauce
1 lb. Medium Onions	²/₃ cup Sherry
Salt	Vinegar

METHOD

❧ Thoroughly wash the cucumber, core the apples, peel the onions, and slice them all very thinly.

❧ In wide-necked jars, layer all three alternately, with a pinch of salt and cayenne between each layer, until all are used. Pour some soy sauce and sherry into each jar and top up with vinegar, ensuring the pickle is completely covered.

FISH SAUCE

Mandrang, or Mandram

This instant pickle is a "West Indian receipt" reported by Eliza Acton. Chop together two cucumbers and one large onion or a small bunch of scallions. Add the juice of a lemon, a teaspoonful of salt, and a pinch or two of cayenne, and mix together with a glass or two of dry white wine. Serve with roast meat, salmon, or pickled fish.

FISH SAUCE TO KEEP

This is based on an anonymous Victorian recipe for a strong, anchovy-based sauce that can be used to spice up soups and stews. Add a small quantity to melted butter to make a creamy fish sauce.

INGREDIENTS

2 Cans of Anchovies in Brine

1 Small Onion

Small Piece of Fresh Horseradish Root, Finely Grated

1 Lemon, sliced

2½ cups White Wine

6 Cloves

²/₃ cup Cold Water

4 T. Walnut Ketchup (see page 14)

METHOD

❧ Drain the anchovies and reserve the liquid. Finely chop the anchovies and onion together. Place all the ingredients, including the anchovy brine but except the walnut ketchup, in a saucepan, and bring to the boil.

❧ Lower the heat to a simmer and continue cooking until the liquid has reduced by approximately half, then strain off the sauce through a muslin and allow to cool completely.

❧ Stir in the walnut ketchup and bottle the sauce in small quantities. Seal well.

ELDERBERRIES MAKE AN UNUSUAL AND
REFRESHING SAUCE FOR OILY FISH

ELDERBERRY KETCHUP

The word catsup
or ketchup comes, in a
roundabout way, from the
Chinese *koechiap* or *ke-tsiap*,
meaning "thick, briny sauce." In Malay,
this became *kechap*. These sauces came
to Europe from South East Asia via
India. As early as 1751, the cook and
restaurateuse Hannah Glasse was
collecting ketchup recipes, and she
remarks of one sauce,

**"It will taste like a
foreign catchup."**

INGREDIENTS

4 cups Ripe Elderberries
1¾ cups Vinegar
2 T. Salt
Small Piece of Root Ginger
¼ cup Black Peppercorns
6 Cloves
Blade of Mace

*T*his unusual recipe is based on Eliza Acton's Pontac Catsup
for Fish, one of her many store sauces. As elderberries
can be gathered for free, this makes a nice, economical
pickle. They have a sweetish, grapey taste that goes
well with oily fish such as mackerel or herring.

METHOD

❧ Thoroughly wash the elderberries and remove any stalks that might
remain. Bring the vinegar to a boil and pour over the berries. Allow it
to stand overnight to infuse.
❧ The following day, strain off the liquid and place it in a saucepan
with the rest of the ingredients; bring to the boil for five minutes and
then allow to cool completely. Do not strain off the spices before
bottling the ketchup.

THE HANSOM CAB

Also known as a four-wheeler, the *"Patent Safety (Hansom) Cab"* was designed and invented in 1834 by Joseph Aloysius Hansom (1803–82), architect and inventor. He also built Birmingham Town Hall, England.

"Excellent!" said Sherlock Holmes. "Send the boy for a four-wheeler, and we shall be off at once..."

ARTHUR CONAN DOYLE, *The Memoirs of Sherlock Holmes*

A SPICY SAUCE FOR CHOPS

Cab Shelter Sauce

When Hansom cabs plied the roads through Victorian London, their drivers gathered in cab shelters, or "cribs," during meal breaks or when trade was slow, to fortify themselves with chops, steaks, eggs, and meat pies. To spice up their meals — and warm themselves after a long drive through a thick, chilly, "pea souper" fog — they invented this dark, piquant, spicy sauce. Each shelter had its own specialized version, but this was the basis.

INGREDIENTS

1 lb. Shallots	2 T. Sugar
1 Clove Garlic	5 t. Mushroom Catsup
1 t. Salt	*(see page 17)*
1 t. Black Pepper	2 cups Vinegar

METHOD

Peel and finely chop the shallots. Place in a saucepan with the all the other ingredients except the vinegar, and cover with cold water. Bring to the boil and cook until the shallots are pulpy.

Remove from the heat and press the contents of the pan through a sieve. To complete the sauce, stir the shallot pulp into the vinegar, and bottle. It is advisable to shake the bottle before each use.

The nectarine
and the curious peach
Into my hands themselves do reach
Stumbling on melons, as I pass,
Ensnared with flowers,
I fall on grass.

Andrew Marvell,
The Garden

FRESH PEACHES MAKE A DELICIOUS FRUITY PICKLE

PICKLED PEACHES

This is an adaptation of Eliza Acton's recipe; it produces a tangy, sour-sweet pickle. These Pickled Peaches are the basis for Peach Mangoes, but are delicious as they are.

INGREDIENTS

6 Under-ripe Peaches
¼ cup Salt
3¾ cups Vinegar
½ Whole White Peppercorns

Small Piece of Root Ginger
2t Salt
½ cup Mustard Seed
⅛ cup Cayenne Pepper
Fresh Water

METHOD

 Mix the salt with 2½ cups of cold water. Wipe the peaches and place them in the solution. Leave them to steep in the liquid for three days then remove and drain thoroughly before packing into a wide-mouthed jar. Place all the spices in a square of muslin and tie tightly.

 Place in a saucepan and pour over the vinegar. Bring to the boil then reduce to a simmer for ten minutes.

 Remove the muslin bag and pour the boiling vinegar over the peaches. Seal tightly and leave for 2 months before using.

SWEET PICKLE OF MELON

This is based on one of Eliza Acton's "foreign receipts." She recommended that it be served with roast meats instead of redcurrant jelly. It is ready to eat in a month from making.

INGREDIENTS

1 Slightly Under-Ripe Cantaloupe Melon
2½ cups Distilled Vinegar

Cloves
1½ cups Sugar
Fresh Water

METHOD

 Carefully peel the melon and cut in half to remove the seeds. Cut the flesh into ½-inch slices and lay them in a pan. Cover with some of the vinegar and simmer very gently until tender. Remove and allow to drain and cool thoroughly, then place two cloves in each of the slices and put the melon slices into glass jars.

 Boil the sugar with 2 cups of cold water to make a sweet syrup. Allow to cool and pour over the melon.

 Cover and allow the melon to steep in the liquid for seven days, then remove and drain the fruit, and pack into storage jars. Cover with the remaining vinegar and seal tightly.

BURNED ONIONS FOR GRAVY

INGREDIENTS

½ lb. Onions

1¼ cups Cold Water

½ cup Moist Brown Sugar

1¼ cups Tarragon Vinegar (see page 11)

This is an adaptation of a Mrs. Beeton recipe. It is an extremely useful sauce for the pantry; use a little of the mixture to add "instant flavour" to gravies made to go with all meats.

METHOD

❧ Peel the onion and chop finely, put in a saucepan, and cover with the water. Bring to the boil and cook until the onion is soft, then add the sugar and simmer until it has dissolved and turned the contents of the pan a very dark brown.

❧ In a separate pan, boil the vinegar and slowly stir this into the onion mixture. When it is all thoroughly combined, remove from the heat and allow to cool before bottling.

PICKLED ONIONS: STILL THE BEST LOVED PICKLE ON THE TABLE

Pickled Onions

According to Eliza Acton, for the most successful Pickled Onion "you must take the smallest onions that can be procured, just after they are harvested, for they are never in so good a state for the purpose as then." The recipe below, however, is an adaptation of Mrs. Beeton's recipe. The onions are ready to eat within six to eight months after pickling.

> *This is a most simple recipe and very delicious, the onions being nice and crisp.*
>
> MRS. BEETON

INGREDIENTS

3 lb. Pickling Onions
1²/₃ cups Salt
3³/₄ cups Vinegar
½ t. Allspice
½ t. Black Peppercorns

METHOD

❧ Make sure the onions are of roughly even size. Place them unpeeled in a large bowl and make a brine solution with half the salt and sufficient water to completely cover them. Pour over and allow the onions to stand for 12 hours before draining off the liquid.

❧ Peel the onions. Make up another brine solution with the remaining salt and immerse the peeled onions for a further 24 to 36 hours. Remove the onions from the brine and pack into clean, sterilized jars.

❧ Add the allspice and black peppercorns to the remaining cold vinegar and pour into the jars, ensuring that the onions are fully covered. Leave for eight weeks before using.

> ONION'S SKIN, VERY THIN
> MILD WINTER COMING IN
> ONION'S SKIN THICK AND TOUGH
> COMING WINTER COLD AND ROUGH.
>
> *A Gardener's Rhyme, 1893*

PICKLED RED CABBAGE

This is an adaptation of Mrs. Beeton's recipe. You should be able to eat it within a week or so, and it should all be consumed within four to six weeks. Eliza Acton gives a rather simpler recipe, omitting the ginger; she observes haughtily that "some persons merely cover the vegetable with strong unboiled vinegar, but this is not so well."

INGREDIENTS

1 Large Red Cabbage
Salt
5 cups Vinegar
Small Piece of Fresh Root Ginger
¼ cup Whole Black Peppercorns

METHOD

❧ Remove the outer leaves from the cabbage and cut in half to remove the white center stalk. Slice the cabbage very finely and layer it in a bowl with salt strewn between each layer. Leave for 24 hours, then drain off any liquid that has collected and rinse the cabbage thoroughly.

❧ Pour the vinegar into a saucepan and bring to the boil with the gently bruised ginger and black peppercorns. Allow five minutes for the flavors to infuse, then remove from the heat and cool.

❧ Fill clean, sterilized jars with the prepared cabbage, and strain the spice vinegar into the jars, ensuring the cabbage is fully covered.

RED BEETS AND RED CABBAGE: A HINT OF CENTRAL EUROPE AND THE RUSSIAN STEPPE IN THE PICKLE JARS OF ENGLAND

PICKLED BEETROOT

This is based on a recipe from Mrs. Beeton. It is ready to eat within a few days of making, yet keeps for several months. Its glorious color makes it an attractive relish on the plate and it is delicious with rye bread and cheese, or dark meats, such as hare.

INGREDIENTS

3lb. Beetroot
2½ cups Vinegar
2 T. Black Peppercorns
¼ cup Allspice

METHOD

❧ Wash the beetroot thoroughly, but be careful not to damage the outer skin, as the beetroot will "bleed" during cooking and loose its beautiful, deep red color.

❧ Place the clean red beet in a saucepan and cover with fresh, cold, lightly salted water. Cook for about two hours or until tender, remove from the water and allow to cool. Peel and slice into ½-inch rounds and pack into clean, sterilized jars.

❧ Boil the peppercorns and allspice with the vinegar for ten minutes. Leave to cool. When cold, fill the prepared jars to the neck and seal.

THE NASTURTIUM

The nasturtium (*Tropaeolum majus*) is both ornamental and useful. The young leaves and flowers are pungent and can be used to enliven a green salad. The flowers – which appear from June to September – make very striking garnishes to sweet and savory dishes. The seed pods can be pickled for winter use.

PICKLED NASTURTIUMS

Pickled Nasturtiums, very popular during the 18th and 19th centuries, are an unusual treat today. Both Mrs. Beeton and Eliza Acton gave recipes, but these were simply formal versions of country recipes. Pickled nasturtium pods can be cooked like capers, to make a piquant sauce for boiled lamb or fish. In Mrs. Beeton's time, nasturtium pods were available to buy in stores, but you would probably have to pick your own today.

INGREDIENTS

Nasturtium Pods
2½ cups Vinegar
⅛ cup Salt
A Few Peppercorns

METHOD

❧ Collect the nasturtium pods on a dry day as soon as possible after the flowers have dropped. The pods should still be green. Carefully wipe them clean, then put them into a clean glass jar. If you feel you have not collected enough to make a good quantity of pickle, do not worry, because you can simply add them to the jar when more become available.

❧ Dissolve the salt in the vinegar and add the peppercorns. Fill the jar of nasturtium pods and seal. They will need several months in the pickling vinegar before they are ready to use.

BRIGHT, HOT-TASTING NASTURTIUMS MAKE
AN UNUSUAL AND INTRIGUING PICKLE

POTTED LOBSTER

ᔕᕆᕊ

This is based on Eliza Acton's recipe. She meant it to eaten immediately, but it will keep for a day or so in the refrigerator. You can use the lobster-coral (roe), rubbed through a sieve, to color the white meat a pearly pink. Alternatively, Eliza Acton suggests that you color only one half of the meat pink, and layer it in a mold with the white meat to produce a beautiful striped dish at the dinner table.

INGREDIENTS

2 Fresh Boiled Lobsters

1 cup Cooked, Peeled Shrimp

¾ cup Butter

Freshly Ground Black Pepper

Pinch of Grated Nutmeg

Butter for Clarifying

ᔕᕆᕊ

METHOD

❦ Remove all the flesh from the lobster and pound with the peeled shrimp, butter and seasoning of nutmeg and a twist of black pepper in a mortar and pestle. As lobster has a delicate taste, it is better to err on the conservative side with the seasoning.

❦ Place the mortar in the refrigerator for an hour or so before potting the lobster mixture, as this will allow it to firm up.

❦ Transfer the lobster paste to small pots. Once potted, melt the butter for clarifying and pass it through a muslin. Pour a little butter over each pot to seal in the lobster's wonderful flavor.

PEELING PRAWNS

Eliza Acton confessed herself surprised that so many people seemed unable to cope with the simple process of peeling prawns or shrimp and ate them with the shells still on, at great danger to their digestion. This is her method: "Unless the fish be stale, when they are apt to break, they will quit the shells easily if the head be held firmly in the right hand and the tail in the other, and the shell of the tail broken by a slight vibratory motion of the right hand, when it will be drawn off with the head adhering to it; a small portion only will then remain on the other end, which can be removed in an instant."

LOBSTER: A LUXURIOUS FOOD FOR SPECIAL OCCASIONS

POTTED CHICKEN

This is based on Eliza Acton's instructions for potting meat. She warns that the meat must be "thoroughly pounded...to the smoothest possible paste, free from a single lump or morsel of unbroken fibre," otherwise the dish will not taste good. Any tender, well-cooked meat can be potted using the same method. Store the Potted Chicken in the refrigerator.

INGREDIENTS

Fresh Chicken weighing 5 lb.
3 cups Butter
Salt and Cayenne for Seasoning
Butter for Clarifying

METHOD

❧ Roast the chicken very thoroughly, so the meat becomes dry and there are no juices left in the flesh. The final dish will last longer if cooked this way.

❧ Remove all the meat from the chicken and chop finely, ensuring there is no skin or bone mixed in. In a mortar and pestle, pound the chopped chicken and softened butter until well amalgamated and season well with salt and cayenne. Pack the chicken mixture into small ceramic pots and lay a fresh bay leaf on top of each one.

❧ Slowly melt the butter for clarifying and pass it through a piece of muslin to remove any impurites. Pour the hot butter over the pots of chicken to seal.

THE HOWLING DESERT MILES AROUND,
THE TINKLING BROOK THE ONLY SOUND
WEARIED WITH ALL HIS TOILS AND FEATS,
THE TRAVELLER DINES ON POTTED MEATS;
ON POTTED MEATS AND PRINCELY WINES,
NOT WISELY BUT TOO WELL HE DINES.

R. L. Stevenson

POTTED CHICKEN: THE FAST FOOD OF THE VICTORIAN TRAVELING CLASSES

BUTTER, CHEESE, AND EGGS FROM THE
FARMHOUSE MAKE SIMPLE, WHOLESOME DISHES.

The auld wife sat by her ivied door
(Butter and eggs and a pound of cheese)
A thing she had frequently done before
And her spectacles lay on her aproned knees.

C S Calverley, **Ballad**

POTTED CHEESE

This is an admirably thrifty way to use up odds and ends of cheese or old cheese that has dried out. It is based on Mrs. Beeton's recipe, which she called Pounded Cheese, and recommended for those with delicate digestions. There are many recipes from old farmhouses for potted cheese. Some add "a glass of sack" – dry white wine or sherry – to the mixture. This Potted Cheese will keep for several days in a cool cupboard, or a week or so in the fridge. To liven up the flavor, a teaspoonful of prepared mustard can be added for each 1lb. of cheese used.

COOK'S TIP

For a more spicy flavor, Mrs. Beeton recommends the addition of cayenne, pounded mace, or curry powder. Use about a teaspoonful to every pound of cheese.

INGREDIENTS

2lb. Cheese

3/4 cup Butter

Butter for Clarifying

METHOD

❦ Cut the cheese and butter into small pieces and pound together in a mortar and pestle until thoroughly mixed together. Pack the mixture into clean jars or ramekins.

❦ Melt the butter for clarifying in a saucepan and strain through muslin. Pour over the pots of cheese to seal.

Being kissed by a man who did not wax his moustache was like eating an egg without salt.

RUDYARD KIPLING, **Soldiers Three**

MANY'S THE LONG NIGHT I'VE DREAMED OF CHEESE – TOASTED, MOSTLY.

Robert Louis Stevenson

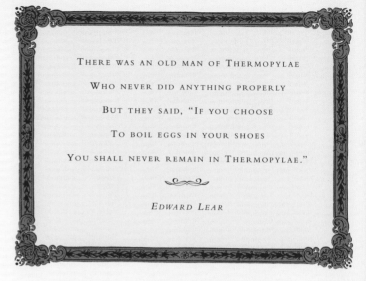

THERE WAS AN OLD MAN OF THERMOPYLAE

WHO NEVER DID ANYTHING PROPERLY

BUT THEY SAID, "IF YOU CHOOSE

TO BOIL EGGS IN YOUR SHOES

YOU SHALL NEVER REMAIN IN THERMOPYLAE."

EDWARD LEAR

PICKLED EGGS

This is based on a recipe of Mrs. Beeton's, but every farmer's wife made Pickled Eggs when her hens had been particularly busy. The eggs are delicious as part of a cold lunch, or for a picnic, or sliced up in salad.

INGREDIENTS

12 Fresh Eggs

3 3/4 cups Vinegar

1/8 cup Black Peppercorns

Small Piece of Fresh Root Ginger

METHOD

❦ Put the eggs in a pan and cover with cold water. Bring to the boil and simmer for 12 minutes. Remove from the heat, plunge into cold water, and take off the shells.

❦ Meanwhile, bring the vinegar to the boil, then simmer it for ten minutes with the peppercorns and root ginger.

❦ Put the eggs into a clean, wide-necked glass jar. Bring the vinegar infusion to the boil once again, then strain over the eggs. Leave to cool and seal tightly. Allow four weeks before eating.

INDEX